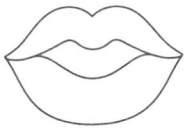

TO: _____

FROM: _____

T0053479

THE HORRORS OF DATING

A COLORING BOOK

ILLUSTRATED BY
NASTKA DRABOT

HARPER Celebrate

The Horrors of Dating
Copyright © 2023 HarperCollins Focus LLC

Cover and interior illustrations: Nastka Drabot

All rights reserved. No portion of this book may be reproduced, stored in a retrieval system, or transmitted in any form or by any means—electronic, mechanical, photocopy, recording, scanning, or other—except for brief quotations in critical reviews or articles, without the prior written permission of the publisher.

Published by Harper Celebrate, an imprint of HarperCollins Focus LLC.

Any internet addresses (websites, blogs, etc.) in this book are offered as a resource. They are not intended in any way to be or imply an endorsement by HarperCollins Focus LLC, nor does HarperCollins Focus LLC vouch for the content of these sites for the life of this book.

ISBN 978-1-4002-4625-0
Wal-Mart Edition 978-1-4041-1983-3

Printed in India

23 24 25 26 27 REP 5 4 3 2 1

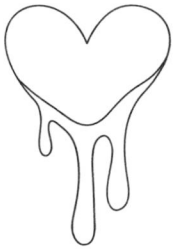

TO THOSE WHO HAVE BEEN BURNED,
HAUNTED, AND GHOSTED LOOKING FOR LOVE,
MAY YOU FIND CATHARSIS IN THESE PAGES.

THE STAGE-FIVE CLINGER

ADDS YOU ON EVERY SOCIAL MEDIA SHE CAN FIND.

THE FINANCE BRO

IN LOVE WITH HIS STOCK PORTFOLIO MORE THAN YOU.

THE
EMOJI
GUY

THE
OUTDOOR
BRO
PEAK ELEVATION,
PEAK DISAPPOINTMENT.

MR.
CROSSFIT
PULLING UP IN YOUR DMS.

THE
BEAST

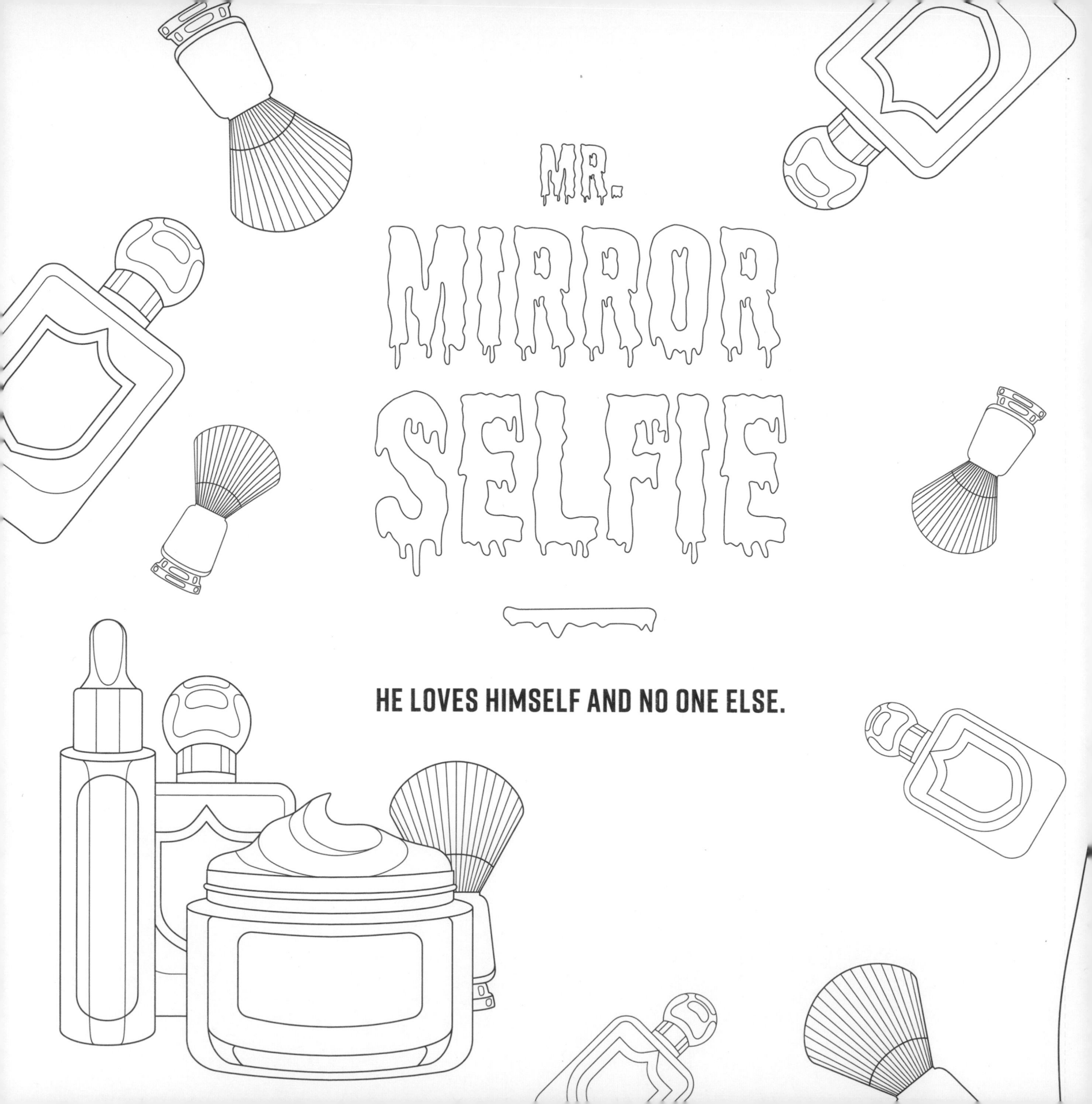
MR.
MIRROR
SELFIE
HE LOVES HIMSELF AND NO ONE ELSE.

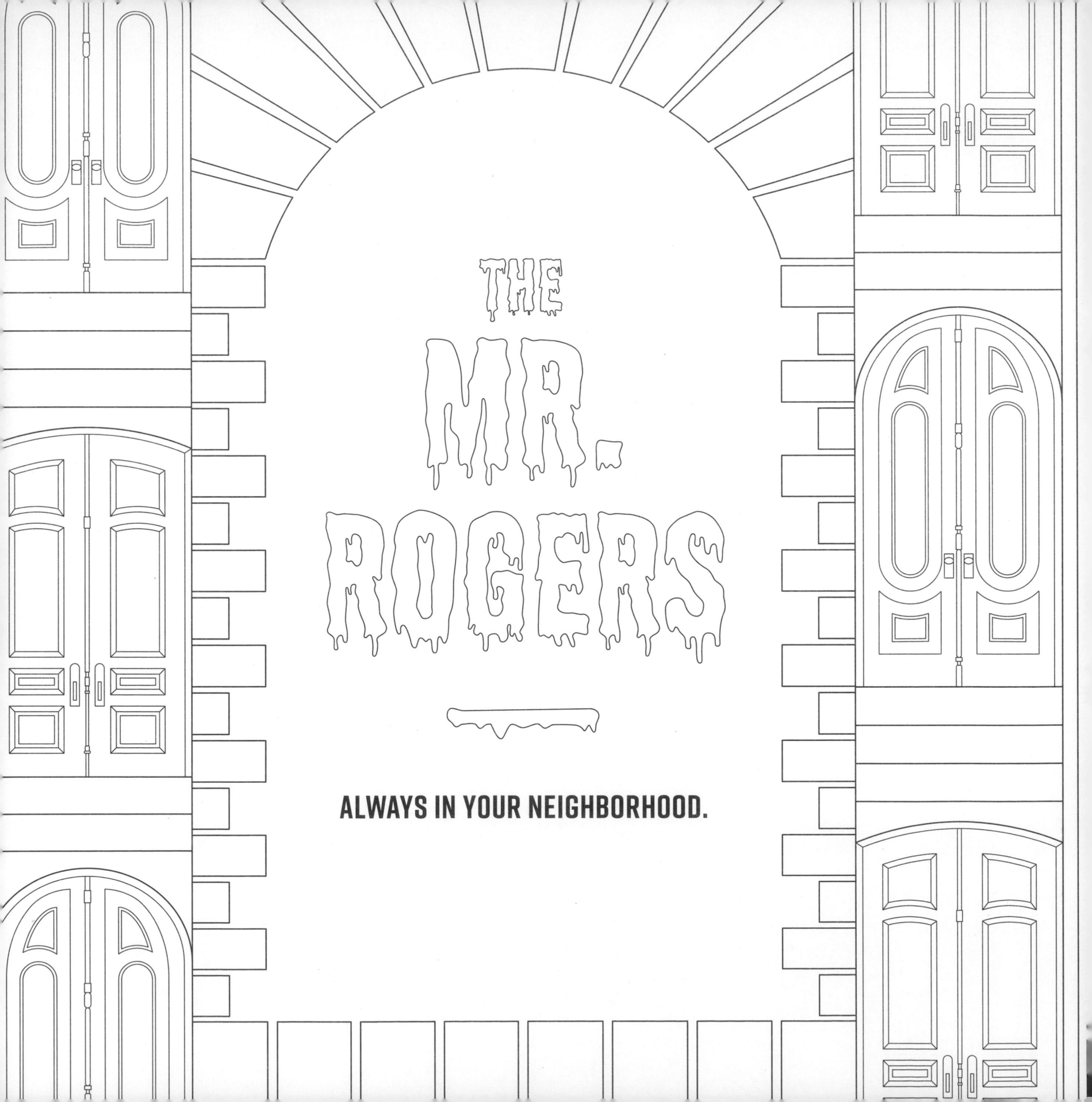
THE
MR.
ROGERS
ALWAYS IN YOUR NEIGHBORHOOD.

THE
GUESS
WHO?
GROUP PHOTOS GALORE . . .
BUT WHICH ONE IS SHE?

THE
FISHERMAN
READY TO HOOK, LINE, AND SINK
(HER INTO DESPAIR).

HAT
GIRL
WHY DO THEY ALL
WEAR THE SAME DANG HAT?

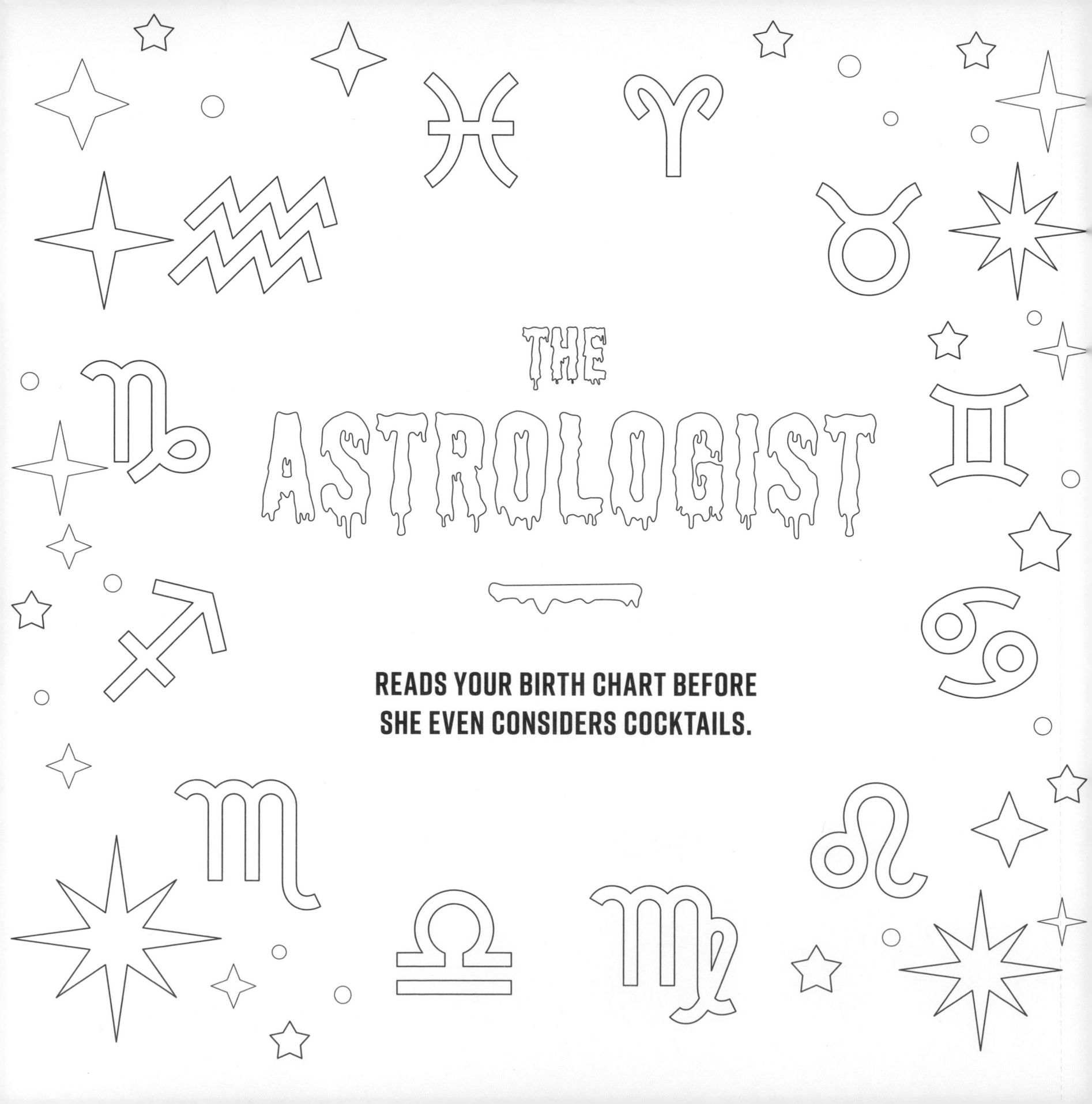
THE
ASTROLOGIST
READS YOUR BIRTH CHART BEFORE
SHE EVEN CONSIDERS COCKTAILS.

THE
GHOSTER
AT LEAST YOU HAVE SOME TIME TO YOURSELF?

THE
SEQUEL
JUST WHEN YOU THINK YOU'RE OUT,
THEY PULL YOU BACK IN.

A NEW
NICE GUY
RETURN
OF
THE NICE
GUY
GUY
TRIKES
BACK

THE
SWIFTIE
SHE'S THE PROBLEM, IT'S HER.

THE INFLUENCER

ONLY DATING YOU FOR THE VIEWS AND THE LIKES.

THE
BACHELORETTE
WANNABE
SHE'S IN IT FOR THE WRONG REASONS.

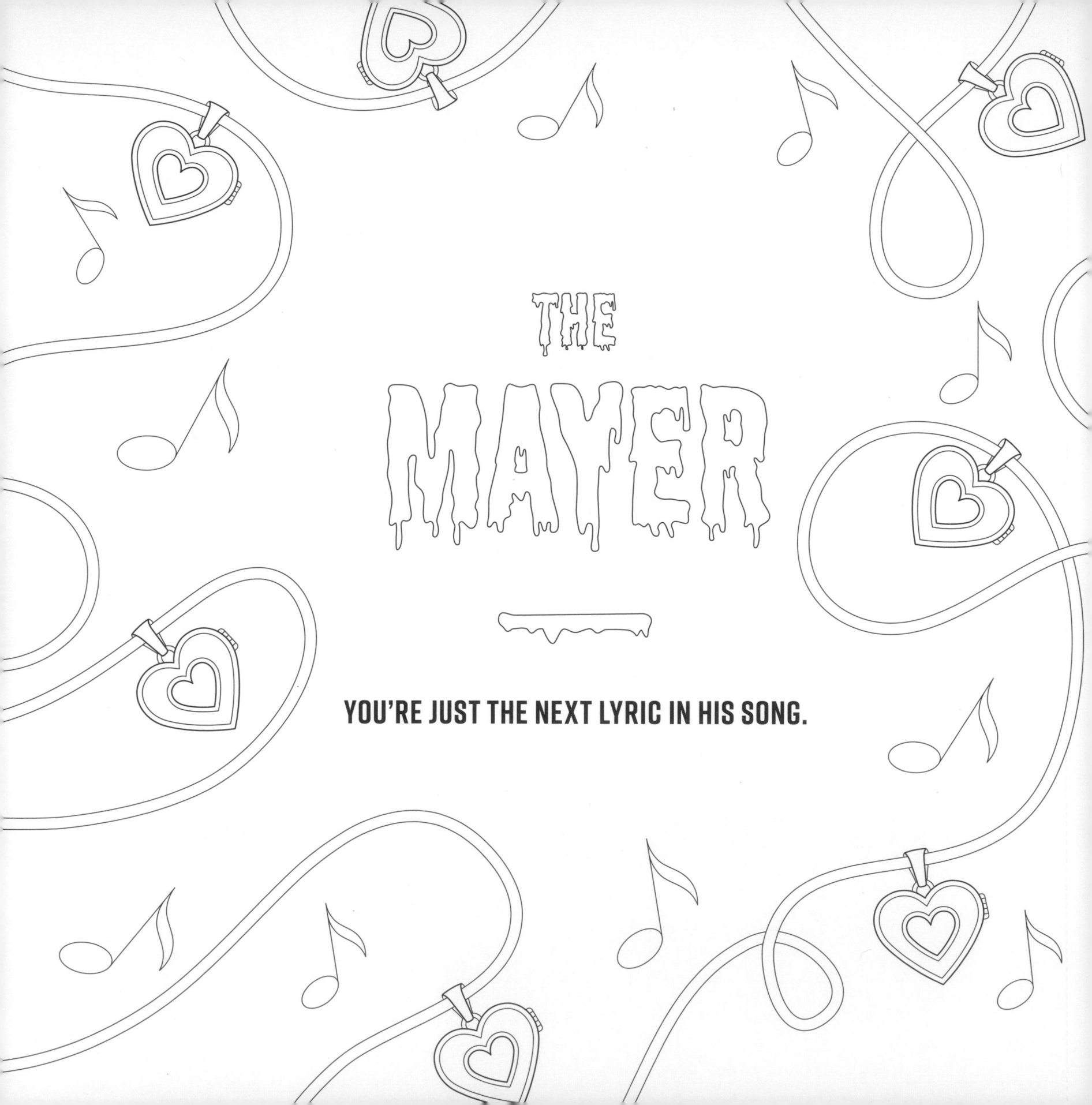
THE
MAYER
YOU'RE JUST THE NEXT LYRIC IN HIS SONG.

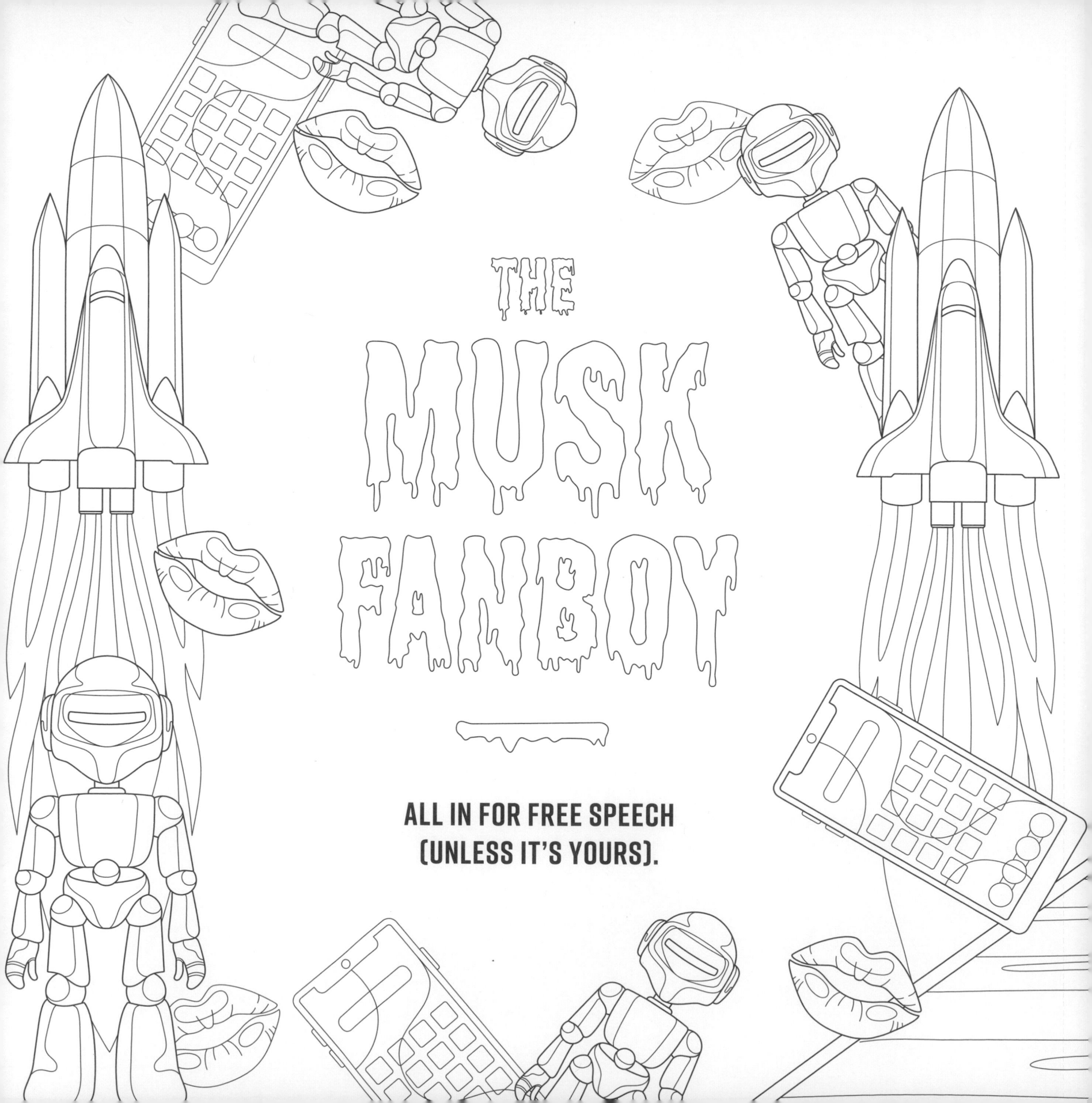
THE
MUSK
FANBOY
ALL IN FOR FREE SPEECH
(UNLESS IT'S YOURS).

TRUTH DAILY
MY THOUGHTS ON THE FUTURE OF EVERY-THING

MRS.
FILL IN THE
BLANK
READY TO COMMIT TO
ANY LAST NAME SHE CAN.

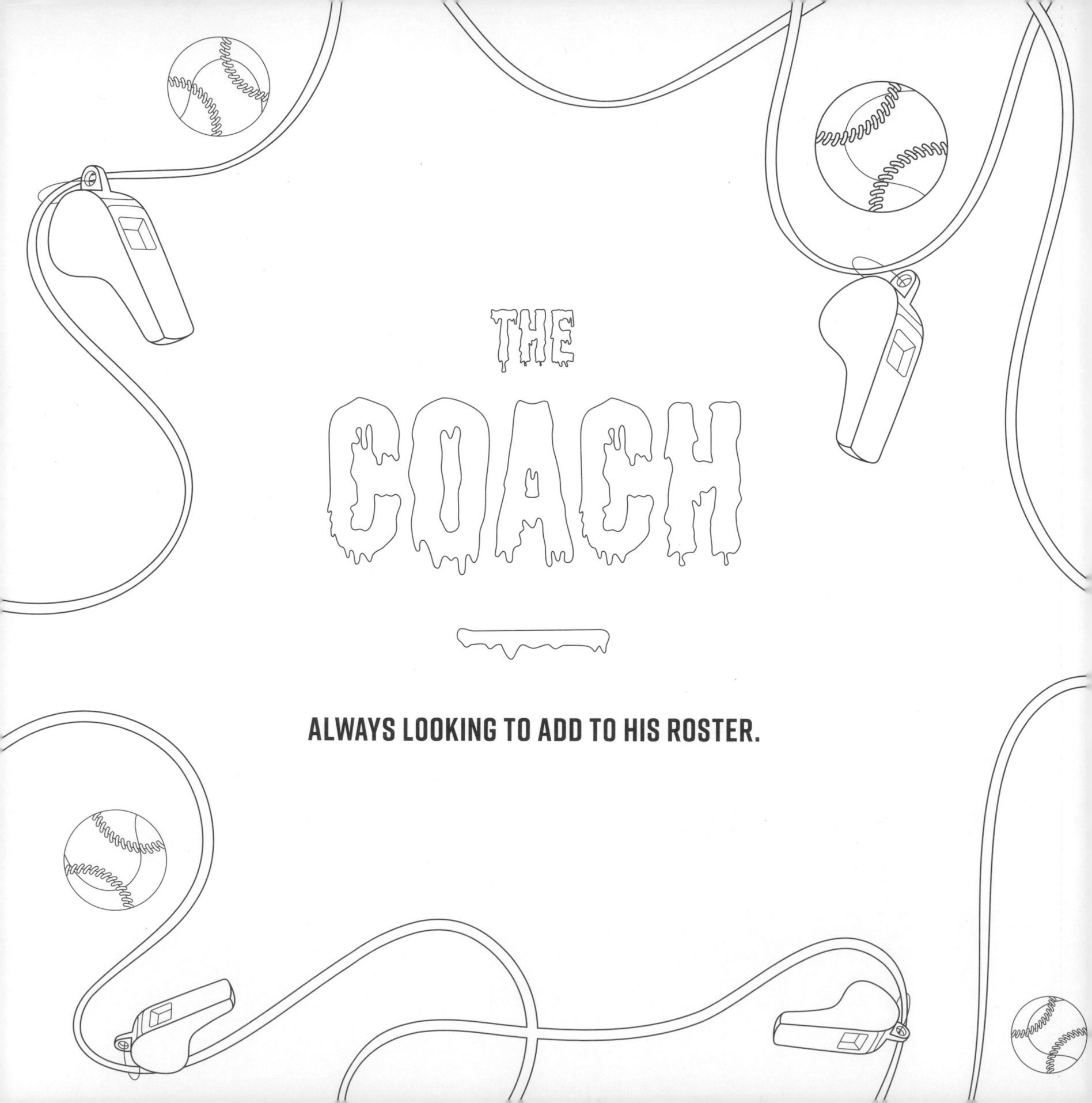
THE
COACH
ALWAYS LOOKING TO ADD TO HIS ROSTER.

1 KATIE
2 JUDY
3 STACY
4 MACY
5 JESS
6 JENNY
7 BELLA

THE
ROYAL
LOOKING FOR A LOYAL SUBJECT
TO WAIT ON HIM HAND AND FOOT.

THE
SELF-EMPLOYED
CEO
SO, I'M HEARING NO BENEFITS.
HELP YOURSELF
YOU'RE SO HOT:
100 REASONS WHY
HUSTLE
FINDING VALIDATION IN MY WORK
BECAUSE I CAN'T FIND IT IN MY
RELATIONSHIPS
WINNING

GRIND
PUT IN THE WORK
HUSTLE
CEO

THE
JET-SETTER
TELL ME MORE ABOUT THAT SEMESTER
ABROAD TEN YEARS AGO!

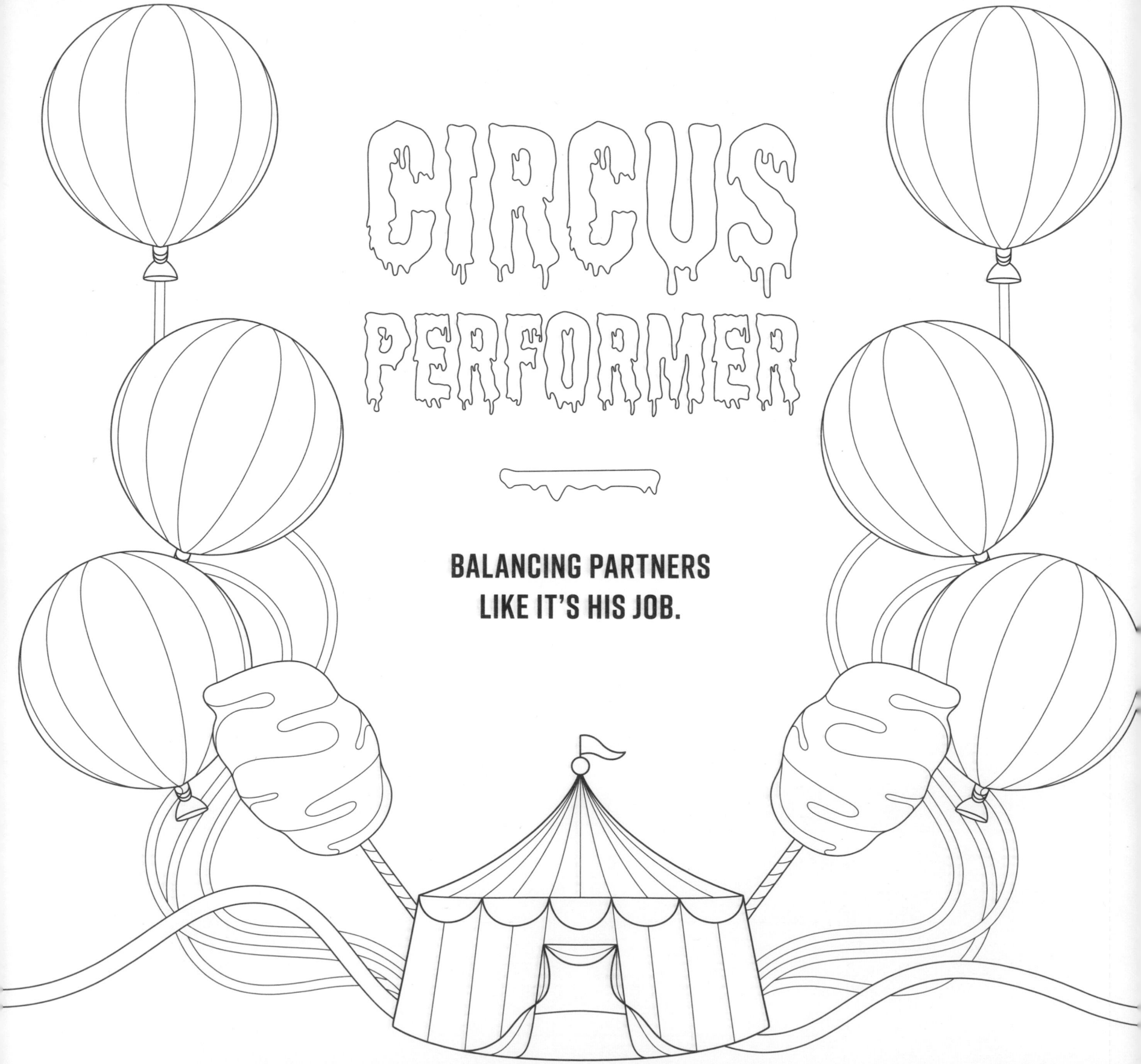
CIRCUS
PERFORMER
BALANCING PARTNERS
LIKE IT'S HIS JOB.

THE PHILOSOPHY GRAD

WHAT A CREATIVE WAY TO SAY UNEMPLOYED WITH STUDENT DEBT!

THE
NOVELIST
SO MANY WORDS.
SO, SO, SO MANY.

THE CABLE NEWS ADDICT

I KNOW YOU FEAR THE COLLAPSE OF SOCIETY AS WE KNOW IT, BUT CAN WE PLEASE JUST EAT THESE COOKIES IN PEACE?

BREAKING NEWS!!!
BREAKING NEWS!!!
BREAKING NEWS!!!

THE
NETWORKER
LINKEDIN IS *NOT* A DATING APP, FULL STOP.

MR.
TOO MUCH,
TOO SOON
NO TALKING ABOUT CHILDREN
ON THE FIRST DATE, THANKS.

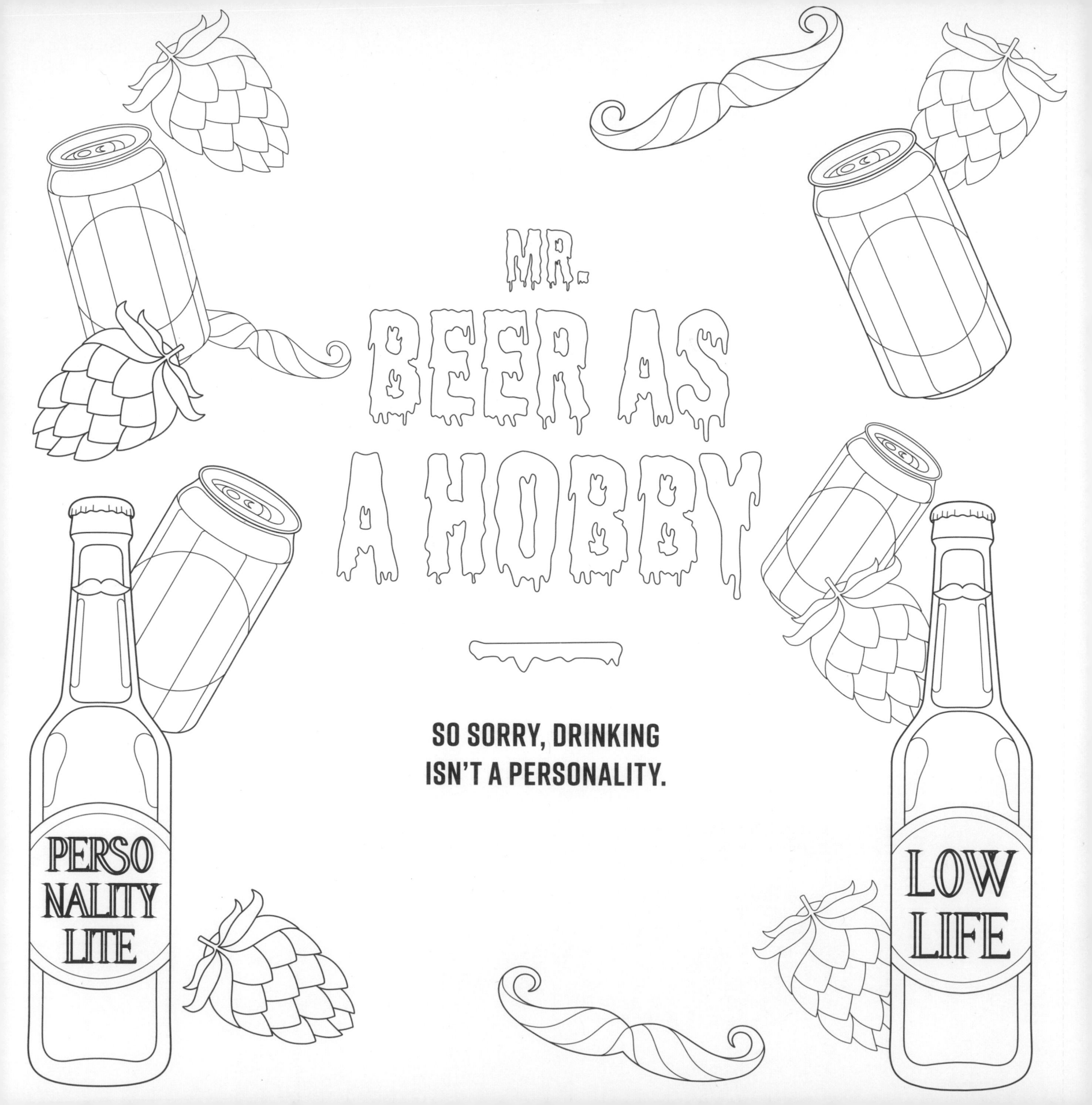
MR.
BEER AS
A HOBBY
SO SORRY, DRINKING
ISN'T A PERSONALITY.
PERSO
NALITY
LITE
LOW
LIFE

THE TIME TRAVELER

I SEE YOUR FRESHMAN YEAR PHOTOS, BUT WHAT DO YOU LOOK LIKE NOW?

GOLDILOCKS
NOTHING IS EVER *JUST RIGHT*.

THE
VULTURE
CIRCLING THE PARTY FOR THE
RICHEST GUY SHE CAN FIND.

THE
LAWYER
SHE'S ALWAYS PUTTING YOU ON TRIAL.

THE KNIGHT IN SHINING ARMOR

NO ONE WAS IN DISTRESS
UNTIL HE SHOWED UP.

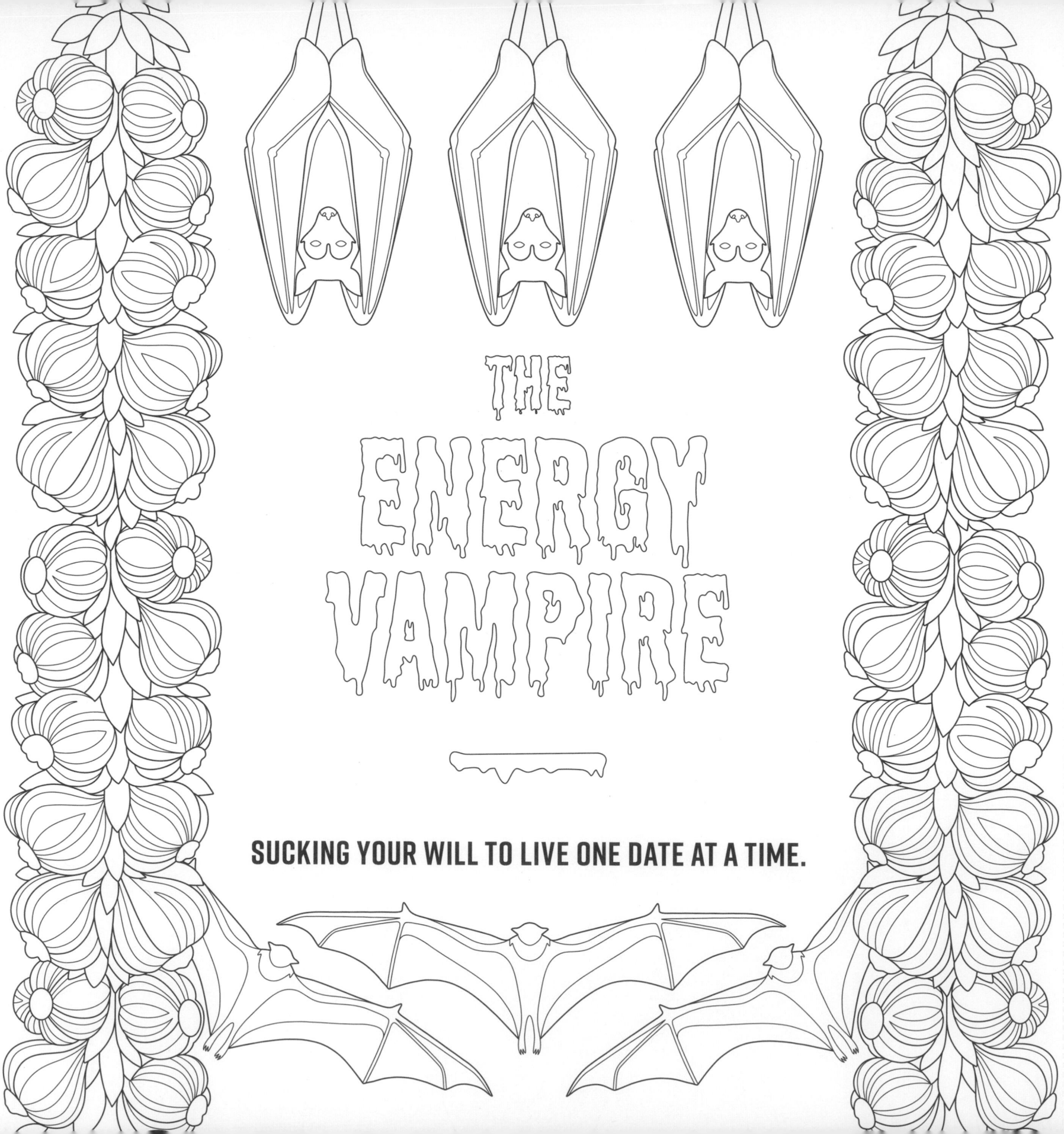
THE
ENERGY
VAMPIRE
SUCKING YOUR WILL TO LIVE ONE DATE AT A TIME.

THE
BOOMERANG
OH MY GOSH, WHY DO YOU
KEEP COMING BACK?

THE
SUN
MY LIFE DOESN'T, IN FACT,
REVOLVE AROUND YOU, BABE.

FORTUNE TELLER

HAS A VISION FOR YOUR FUTURE TOGETHER BEFORE YOU EVEN TELL HER YOUR LAST NAME.

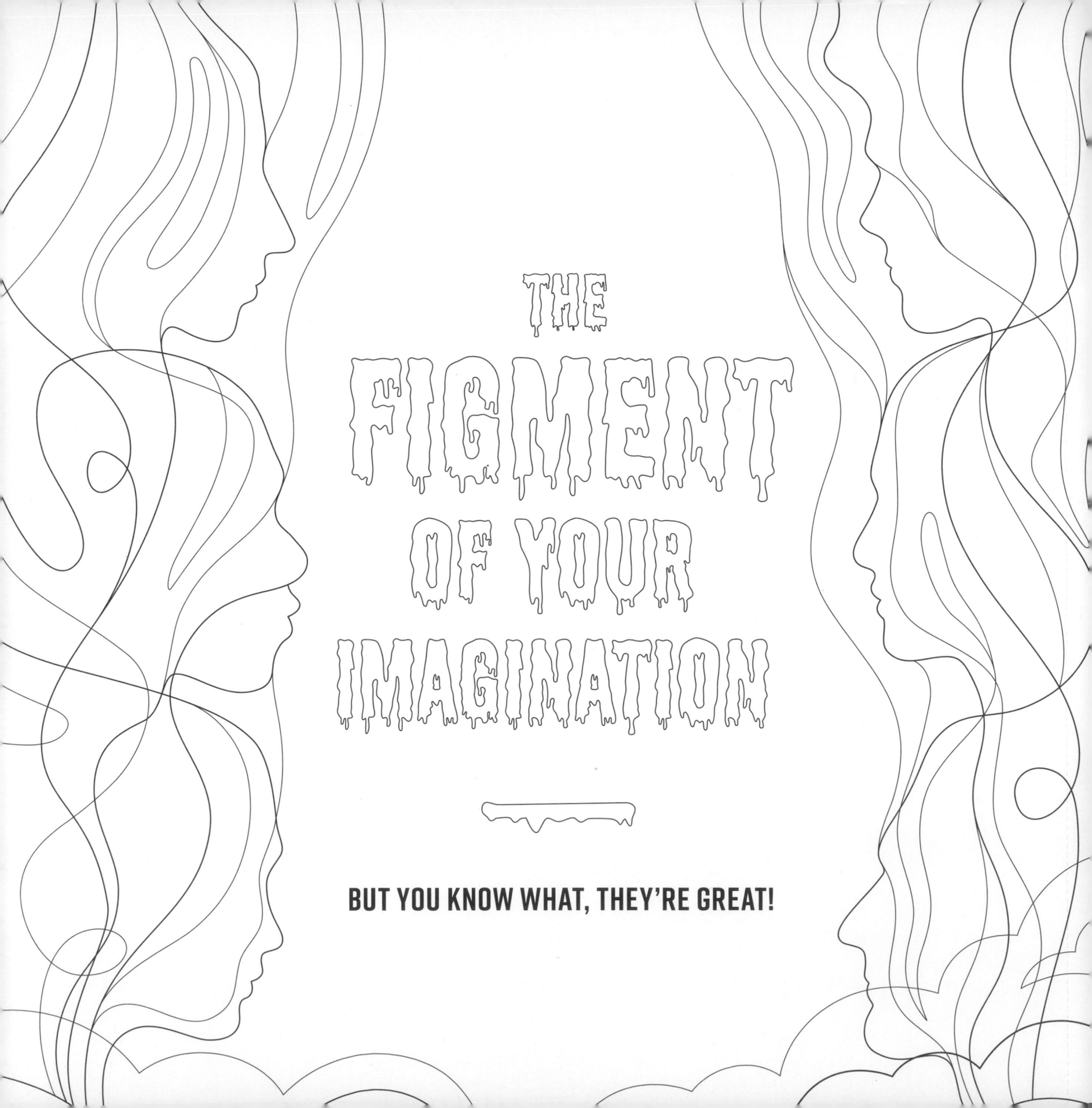
THE
FIGMENT
OF YOUR
IMAGINATION
BUT YOU KNOW WHAT, THEY'RE GREAT!

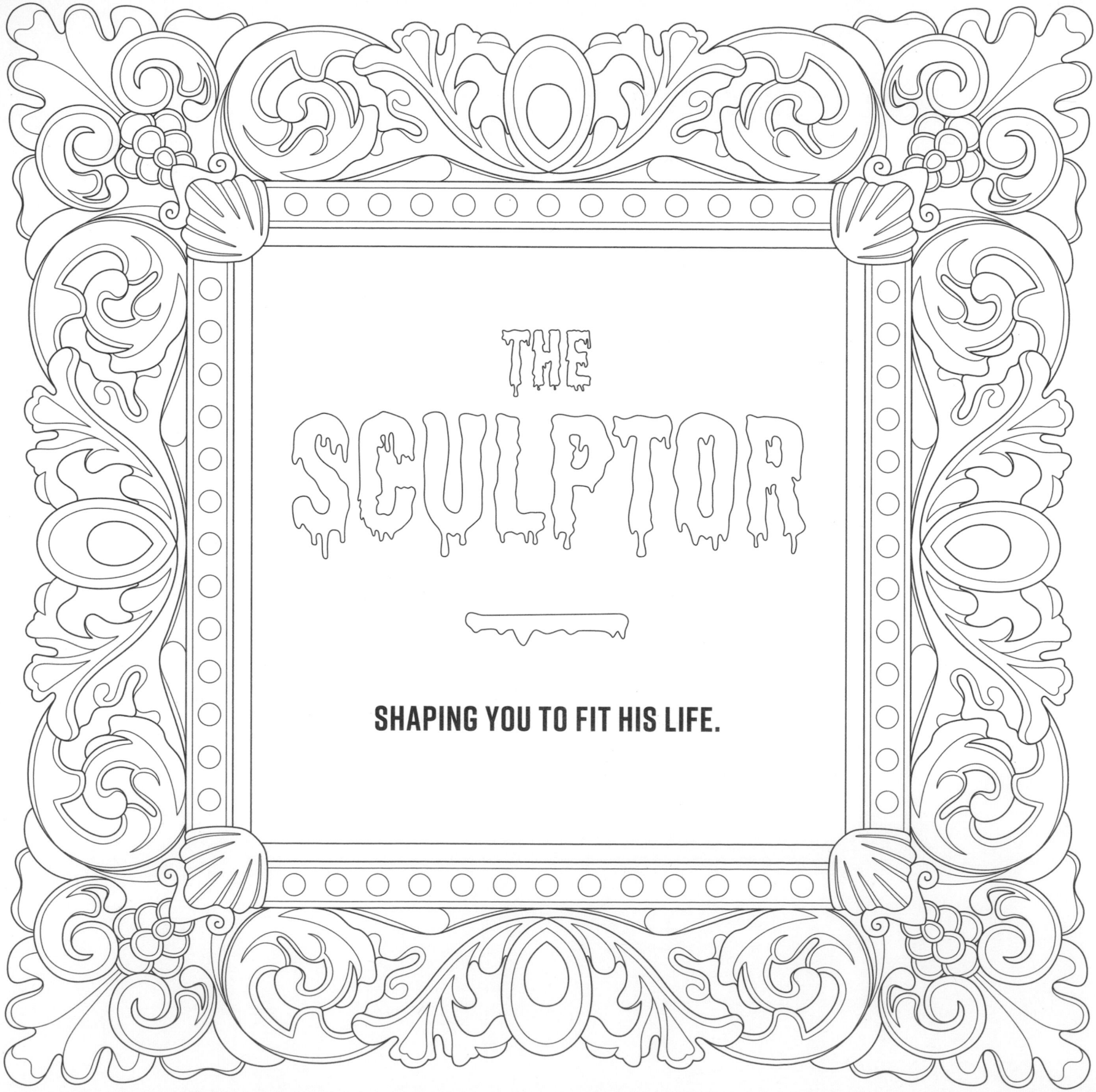
THE
SCULPTOR
SHAPING YOU TO FIT HIS LIFE.

THE
JANE
AUSTEN
LOOKING FOR HER DARCY,
BUT THE THING IS,
SHE'S NO ELIZABETH.

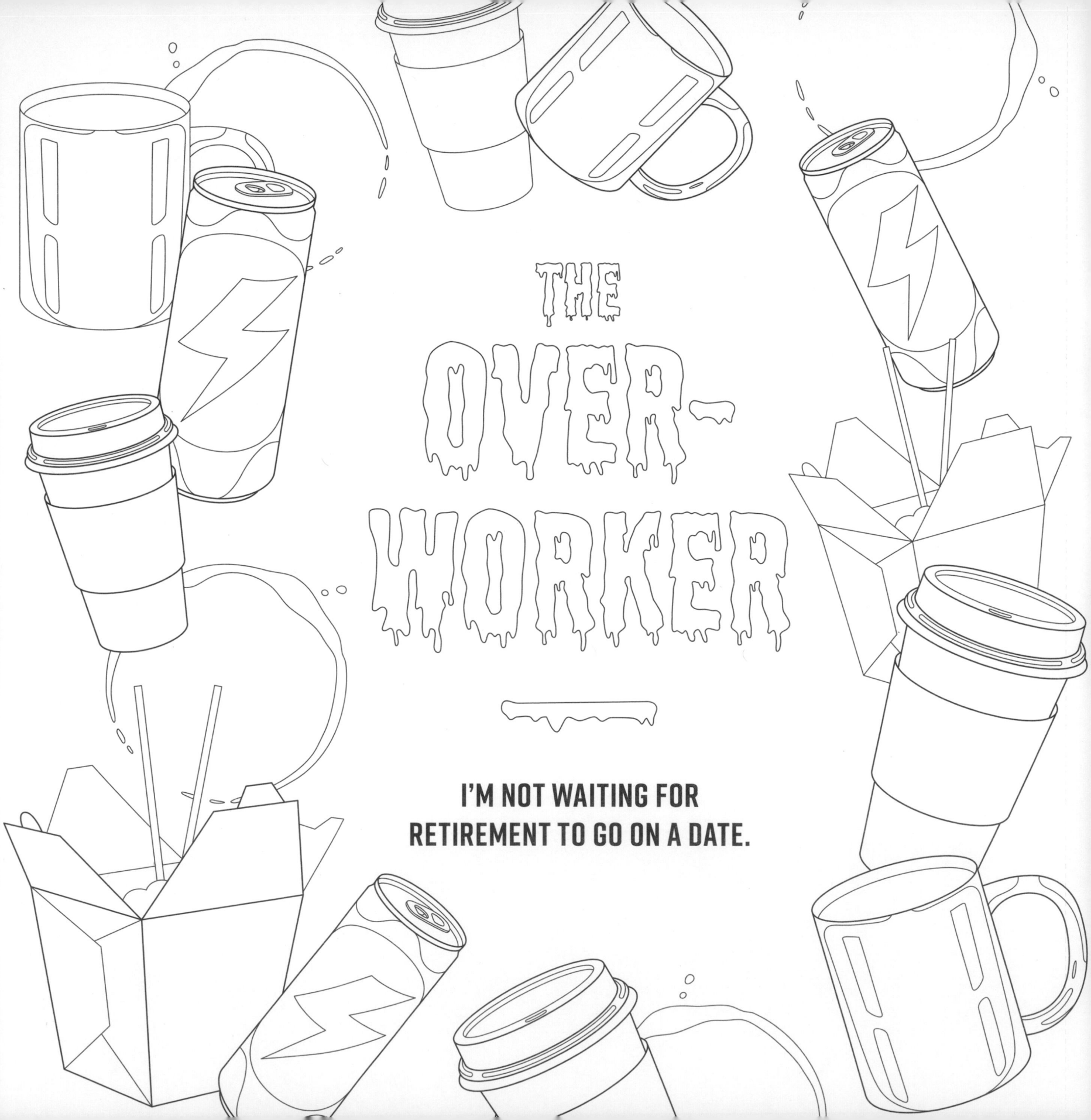
THE
OVER-
WORKER
I'M NOT WAITING FOR
RETIREMENT TO GO ON A DATE.

THE
QUARTERBACK
I MEAN, COOL?

MOM'S COOKIES
MOM
THE FREUDIAN SLIP
MOM
MOM'S CASSEROLE
MOM
NO, I DON'T COOK LIKE YOUR MOM,
AND NO, I WON'T APOLOGIZE.
MOM'S POT ROAST
MOM

MOM

TO ALL MY EXES . . .
BITE ME